BUILDING A

CAR

BY DANIELLE S. HAMMELEF

CONTENT CONSULTANT
WADE BARTLETT, PE,
MECHANICAL FORENSICS
ENGINEERING SERVICES, LLC
ROCHESTER, NEW HAMPSHIRE

READING CONSULTANT
BARBARA J. FOX
PROFESSOR EMERITA
NORTH CAROLINA STATE UNIVERSITY

CAPSTONE PRESS
a capstone imprint

Blazers Books are published by Capstone Press,
1710 Roe Crest Drive, North Mankato, Minnesota 56003
www.capstonepub.com

Library of Congress Cataloging-in-Publication Data
Hammelef, Danielle S., author.
  Building a car / by Danielle S. Hammelef.
      pages cm — (Blazers books. See how it's made.)
  Summary: "Describes the process of building a car"—Provided by publisher.
  Includes bibliographical references and index.
  Audience: 4-6.
  Audience: 8-13.
  ISBN 978-1-4765-3976-8 (library binding)
  ISBN 978-1-4765-5116-6 (paperback)
  ISBN 978-1-4765-5957-5 (eBook pdf)
  1. Automobiles—Design and construction—Juvenile literature. I. Title.
  TL240.H295 2014
  629.2'34—dc23   2013026503

Editorial Credits
Mandy Robbins, editor; Kyle Grenz, designer; Kathy McColley, production specialist

Photo Credits
Alamy: Andrew Fox, 19, Caro/Kaiser, 22, 25, Caro/Ruffer, 26, Justin Kase zsixz, 29; Corbis:
Imaginechina, 10; Dreamstime: Derek Miller, 1; Newscom: Getty Images/AFP/Yoshikazu Tsuno, 9;
Science Source: Maximilian Stock Ltd, 20; Shutterstock: Evgeny Korshenkov, cover (background),
lexan, 5, Nikkolia, cover, 1 (inset laser), Rainer Plendl, 16, Rob Wilson, cover, sparkdesign, throughout
(background), Vereshchagin Dmitry, 12, withGod, 6, zhu difeng, 15

Printed in the United States of America in Stevens Point, Wisconsin.
092013   007768WZS14

TABLE OF CONTENTS

DESIGNING CARS
PART BY PART 4

TESTING CAR
DESIGNS. 8

PUTTING THE
PARTS TOGETHER 14

FINISHING TOUCHES. 24

FROM FACTORY
TO DEALERSHIP 28

GLOSSARY. 30
READ MORE 31
INTERNET SITES 31
INDEX 32

CHAPTER 1

DESIGNING CARS PART BY PART

Every car has thousands of parts, from tiny wires to heavy engines. Before a new car hits the road, each part must fit together like a puzzle.

FACT
German inventor Karl Benz built the first car in 1885. He called his three-wheeled gasoline-powered car a Motorwagen.

MAJOR CAR BRANDS

Brand	Country of Origin	Year Started
FORD	USA	1903
CHEVROLET	USA	1911
DODGE	USA	1914
BMW	GERMANY	1916
TOYOTA	JAPAN	1924
NISSAN	JAPAN	1933
VOLKSWAGEN	GERMANY	1937
HONDA	JAPAN	1948
HYUNDAI	SOUTH KOREA	1967

Passat CC

How do cars go from a concept to a shiny new car? The process takes about five years and hundreds of people. Each piece is specially designed. Workers choose materials such as metals, plastics, and glass to make each part.

concept—an idea for a new way to build or design something

CHAPTER 2

TESTING CAR DESIGNS

Car designers use computers to turn ideas into three-dimensional drawings. Computers help designers plan for the best body shape and type of engine. After the computer tests, life-size clay models are built.

three-dimensional—having or appearing to have length, depth, and height

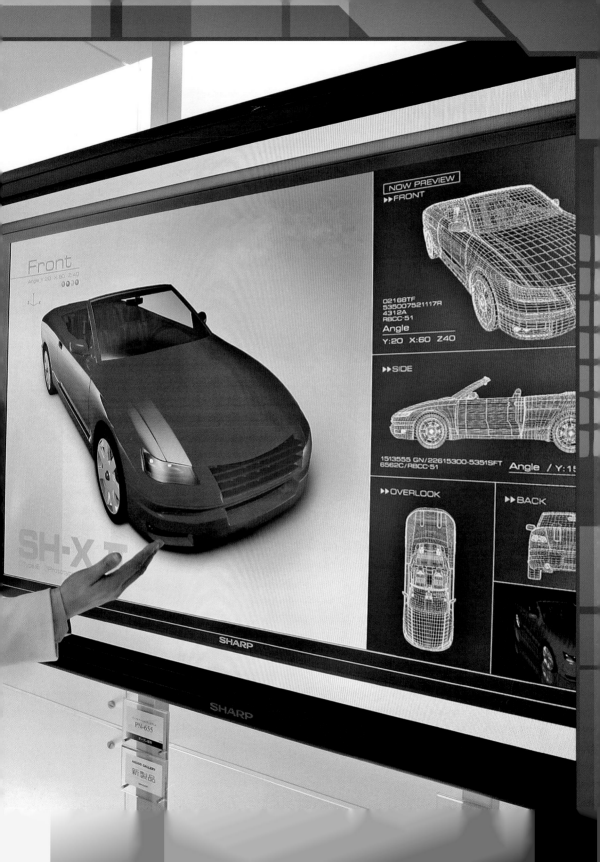

Teams spend hundreds of hours testing prototypes. Workers test prototypes in a wind tunnel. They use test results to change the car's shape so it cuts through the air more easily.

prototype—the first version of an invention that tests an idea to see if it will work
wind tunnel—a tunnel through which air is blown to study airflow around an object

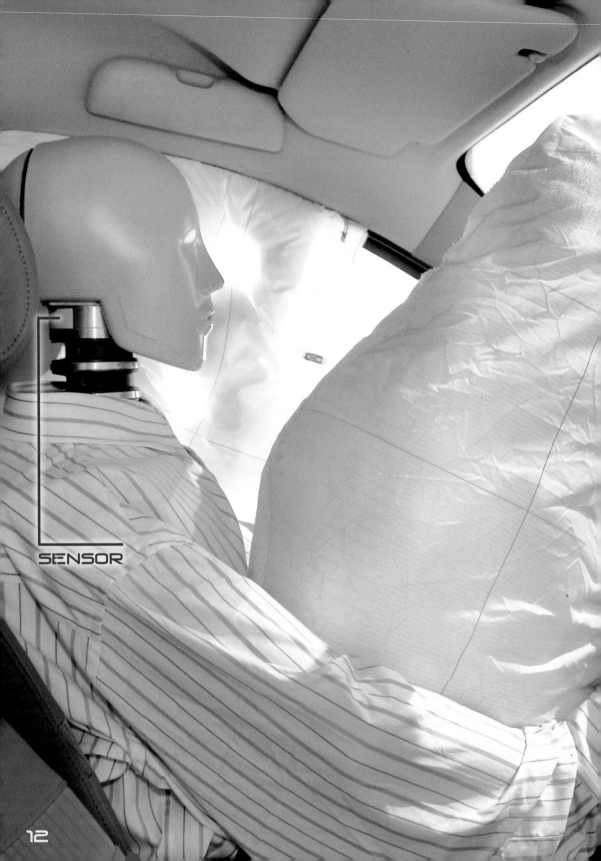

SENSOR

Prototypes go through crash tests to check the safety of new designs. Engineers make changes so cars are as safe as possible. They make dashboards softer and move engine parts. They make other parts break easier during a crash.

FACT
Crash test dummies have sensors. Sensors show whether people may break bones or suffer head injuries during an accident.

engineer—a person who uses science and math to plan, design, or build

CHAPTER 3

PUTTING THE PARTS TOGETHER

Once a prototype gets approved, factories make thousands of parts. Steel is a metal that makes up many parts of a car. **Foundry** workers use **metal castings** to make engines. **Metal stamping** plants make doors, hoods, and roofs. Other factories make plastic parts.

foundry—a factory for melting and shaping metal
metal casting—liquid metal that is poured into a hollow mold and allowed to cool and harden
metal stamping—the pressing of sheet metal into a particular s

14

ST 430

Robots do dangerous and
repetitive jobs at the factory. They
move heavy parts and lift cars onto
the assembly line. Robots work with
high heat when they weld the car
body shells together.

assembly line—a group of workers and machines that puts
   products together; products pass from one station to the next
   until the job is done
weld—to join two pieces of metal by heating them until they
   melt together

Workers smooth bumps on metal car body shells. They clean dirt and oils off it. The shells are dipped in giant tubs full of primer. Large ovens bake the primer. Robots use spray arms to apply several coats of paint.

primer—a coat of paint that goes on before the main color to make the paint stick better

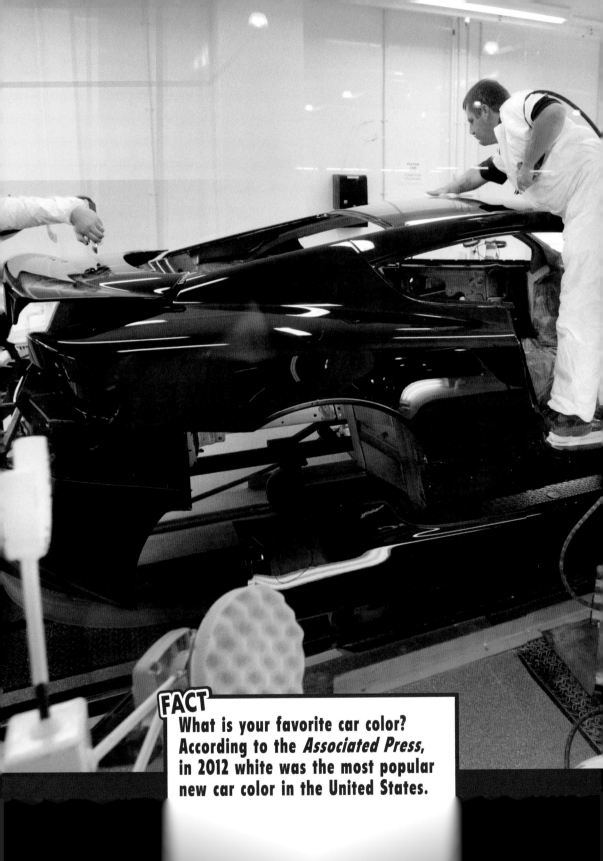

FACT
What is your favorite car color?
According to the *Associated Press*,
in 2012 white was the most popular
new car color in the United States.

Engines arrive at the factory as empty metal cases. Factory workers add **pistons**, **spark plugs**, and other engine parts.

piston—part of an engine that moves up and down within a tube called a cylinder

spark plug—one of the parts of a gasoline engine that supplies an electrical spark to ignite the fuel and air mixture in a cylinder

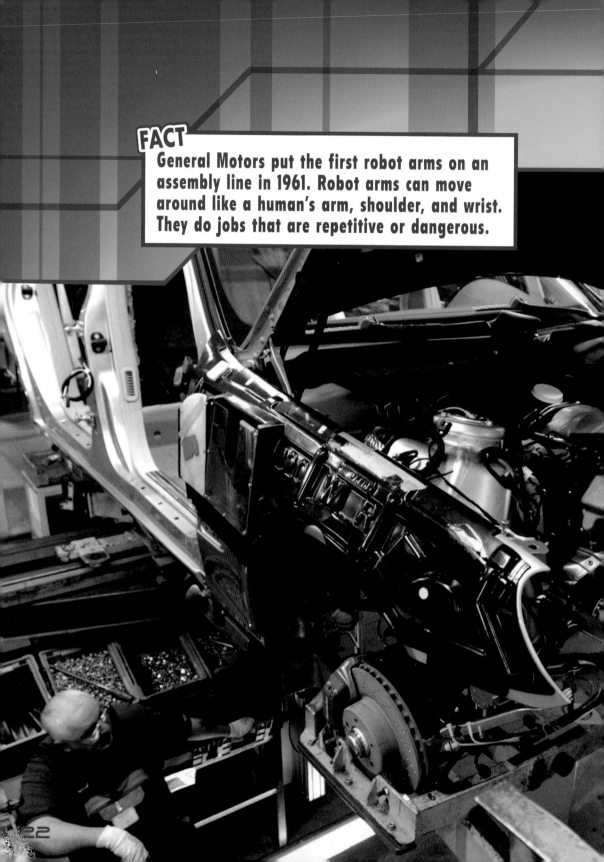

General Motors put the first robot arms on an assembly line in 1961. Robot arms can move around like a human's arm, shoulder, and wrist. They do jobs that are repetitive or dangerous.

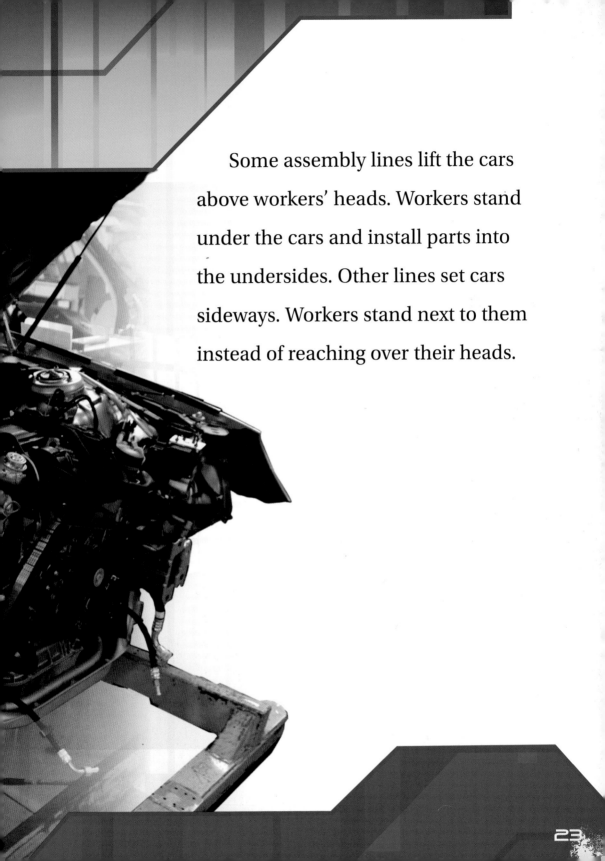

Some assembly lines lift the cars above workers' heads. Workers stand under the cars and install parts into the undersides. Other lines set cars sideways. Workers stand next to them instead of reaching over their heads.

CHAPTER 4

FINISHING TOUCHES

Once the working parts are in place, workers install body panels and doors. They connect dashboards, lights, batteries, and seats. They fill the gas tank and add engine oil and brake fluid.

FACT
In 2012 car factories built more than 60 million cars worldwide.

Before a car can leave the factory, workers test it. They start the engines. They test brakes, radios, headlights, and horns. Workers test drive completed cars or place them on a dynamometer.

dynamometer—a machine similar to a treadmill used to test vehicles; a dynamometer measures power

CHAPTER 5

FROM FACTORY TO DEALERSHIP

Once cars pass final tests, workers drive them onto large trucks, trains, or ships. The cars are delivered to dealerships where people can buy them. What car would you like to drive home?

GLOSSARY

assembly line (uh-SEM-blee LINE)—a group of workers and machines that puts products together

concept (KON-sept)—an idea for a new way to build or design something

dynamometer (dy-nuh-MAH-mih-tuhr)—a machine similar to a treadmill used to test vehicles; a dynamometer measures power

engineer (en-juh-NEER)—a person who uses science and math to plan, design, or build

foundry (FOUN-dree)—a factory for melting and shaping metal

metal casting (MET-uhl CASS-ting)—liquid metal that is poured into a hollow mold and then allowed to cool and harden

metal stamping (MET-uhl STAM-ping)—the pressing of sheet metal into a particular shape

piston (PISS-tuhn)—part of an engine that moves up and down within a tube called a cylinder

primer (PRY-mur)—a base coat of paint that goes on before the main color to make the paint stick better

prototype (PROH-toh-type)—the first version of an invention that tests an idea to see if it will work

spark plug (SPARK PLUG)—one of the parts of a gasoline engine that supplies an electrical spark to ignite fuel and air in a cylinder

three-dimensional (THREE–duh-MEN-shun-uhl)—having or appearing to have length, depth, and height

weld (WELD)—to join two pieces of metal by heating them until they melt together

wind tunnel (WIND TUHN-uhl)—a tunnel through which air is blown to study airflow around an object

READ MORE

Eason, Sarah. *How Does a Car Work?* New York: Gareth Stevens Publishing, 2010.

Economy, Peter. *New Car Design*. Novato, Calif.: Treasure Bay, 2010.

Von Finn, Denny. *Concept Cars*. Minneapolis: Bellwether Media, 2010.

Williams, Brian. *Who Invented the Automobile?* Mankato, Minn.: Arcturus Publishing, 2010.

INTERNET SITES

FactHound offers a safe, fun way to find Internet sites related to this book. All of the sites on FactHound have been researched by our staff.

Here's all you do:

Visit *www.facthound.com*

Type in this code: 9781476539768

INDEX

assembly lines, 17, 22, 23

batteries, 24
Benz, Karl, 4
body panels, 24, 25
brakes, 24, 27

car body shells, 17, 18
concepts, 7
crash test dummies, 13

dashboards, 13, 24
dealerships, 28
designers, 8

engineers, 13
engines, 4, 8, 13, 14, 20, 24, 27

factories, 14, 17, 20, 26, 27
Ford, Henry, 17

gas tanks, 24

lights, 24, 27

materials, 7, 14
metal castings, 14
metal stamping, 14
models, 8

painting, 18
pistons, 20
prototypes, 11, 13, 14

robots, 17, 18, 22

seats, 24
spark plugs, 20

tests, 8, 11, 13, 27, 28

wind tunnels, 11

31901055338711